UNSPOKEN TABOO

Sympol the Poet

I would like to thank my son's,
Tahj and Devaun for always showing me that anything is possible.
I also want to thank my mom for always having my back.
Tara, thank you for all of your assistance in helping
make this book possible.

Always put your trust in God.
Sympol the Poet

Sympol

The Poet

IN MEMORY

Barry

IN MEMORY

Brother

IN MEMORY

Stacy

TABLE OF CONTENTS

THEY CALL ME SYMPOL

They call me Sympol.
It's a metaphor because my poetry is simple but with a few twists and turns.
I'm a complicated man.
Such as a rubic cube is a simple square but with a few twists and turns.
It's complicated to understand.
Just as the pyramids are a simple triangle yet it baffles man to this day.
Such as it's simple to understand prayer,
But you can't fathom how God hears one out of millions when you pray.
Like it's simple to understand that a cow goes moo, a pig goes oink and a duck goes quack,
But it's difficult to understand why a white swan is born to this earth black.
I just want to unite all people...it's that simple, that's all.
I just want to bring all people together like the fall of The Berlin Wall.
There are those of you out there who will get this, and you are on the right path.
And then there are those of you out there who are clueless,
Like a gorilla in the Congo scratching his ass.
So, to put it simple, I'm simply the best!
The person who loves to hear me speak the most...
I found out she's DEAF!
Is that too complicated or is that too simple?
Don't feel simple-minded if that riddle makes you scratch your temple!
That's why they call me Sympol!

I'M A THUG

God's breath blows a leaf off a tree.
It lands on a splinter of grass.
Oh, to hell with that.
I'm a thug!
Let's get this book started!

VOODOO

It's you that I'm pursuing.
I put one foot in front of the other and I start moving.
I'm so close you can smell my cologne.
Damn girl, why can't I leave you alone?
I feel like I'm drugged.
Like I'm in a fog or a daze,
I'm following you around like a puppy in a maze.
Things became clear that night when you invited me to your apartment.
It all made since when I stumbled upon that secret compartment.
There was a doll that strongly resembled me.
There was a picture of me wrapped in a pair of your panties.
Under that secret compartment I found another secret layer.
It contained a chicken bone and wrapped around it was a lock of my hair.
Now I know why I eat, sleep and drink you,
Because literally, you used voodoo.
So, what do I do now that this information has come into my life?
What do I do now that this bitch is my wife?

PRAY

Now I lay me down to sleep.
BANG! BANG! BANG!
I pray the Lord my soul to keep.
BANG! BANG!
If I should die before I wake.
BANG!
I pray the Lord my soul to take.
She grew up surrounded by violence,
She couldn't even say her prayers in silence.
Surrounded by teen pregnancy and prostitution,
Even her family told her "God is just an illusion."
She stayed strong and focused and never held a grudge.
10 years later she's always in court,
But not on trial.
She's the judge.
She still says her prayers night after night,
Only now gunshots don't pierce the sounds of her suburban life.

PRAY!

YOU GO GIRL

Our eyes met from across a crowded room just like in the movies.
She slowly made her way to me so smoothly.
She held out her hand and introduced herself as Celeste.
I fought the urge to grab her ass, kiss her lips, and caress her chest.
Obviously, I kept things classy,
She had a southern drawl, well educated, and just a little bit sassy.
We had such a connection from politics all the way to sports,
She even told me she was the bomb on the basketball court.
She thought I didn't believe that she was a former model,
She was constantly sending me pictures of her radiant face and body like a coke bottle.
It's been two weeks of lunches, brunches, and fine dinners,
I want to keep treating her like an angel, but tonight she wants to be treated like a sinner.
Her business suit came off and she was down to her underwear that were so fancy.
Victoria definitely had a secret that night because a penis came out of her panties.
So that's the burden that I carry.
I told you twice before officer,
I don't know where his/her body is buried.

YOU LAUGH

You laugh because my apartment has one bedroom,
While your bedrooms total four.
You laugh because my car is eight years old,
And your car comes straight off the showroom floor.
I laugh because I have peace of mind,
I laugh because when you were in jail,
I know you took it from behind.
I laugh because your daughter is a stripper,
I laugh because on your lip is a fever blister.
That fever blister came from the man next door,
He gave your wife a sexually transmitted disease because your
wife is a whore.
You may laugh, but I have peace of mind,
I laugh because your third child is actually mine.

OOPS

A year ago, I didn't know where this was heading,
Who would have thought today would be your wedding?
The look written on your face is one of excitement,
At the same time fear because somehow, I was invited.
I had to crash your reception,
If not, this would be a day forever I'd end up regretting.
I managed to sneak you away from the groom,
I managed to sneak you into the back room.
A year ago, we had an affair that made life a mess.
Now on your wedding day you're having sex with me in your
wedding dress.
I guess in nine months we will unite,
Because, oops I didn't wear a condom on your wedding night.

WONDERING

My best friend's riding his bike and I'm on the handlebars,
Seven months later I'm stealing cars.
It's happening so fast,
What's this all about?
Five months later I'm breaking in someone's house.
How fast is this going?
I can't tell.
Three months later I'm robbing Taco Bell.
Where did I go wrong?
I loved going to church with my grandma and listening to gospel
songs.
Maybe it's when she passed,
And my biological mother was in the club shaking her ass.
Even though a couple of years later I was adopted,
The damage was done and sadly I could not stop it.
Inmate #SCB4431

EDGE

I'm unhappy because you make me happy.
I do better in life with a chip on my shoulder,
Let's call it a boulder.
Misery brings out the best in me,
Your love kills my animosity.
Misery loves company.
But not in this case,
I hate the smile you put on my face.
You've turned my sharp edge dull,
I guess I'm not happy unless I'm miserable.
Is it twisted that I wish you would cheat on me?
Is it twisted that I wish you would give me an STD?
Is it twisted that I wish you would cheat with my brother?
Hell, even cheat with my son's mother?
Is it twisted to want the maintenance man to find you dead?
Is it twisted to wish for anything that will give me back my edge?

TWO OF A KIND

Who wanted you?
Who wanted me?
No one on this earth,
And many would agree.
But with me by your side,
And you by mine.
The people who no longer wanted us,
Now admire a love like ours.

I guess you could say,
"Two of a Kind."

WISH

I know that in your past life you think your skin was White,
But in this lifetime your skin is as Black as mine.
Around me and my friends you don't know how to act,
Just because we come from the wrong side of the tracks.
Don't be so quick to look down your nose,
Because I heard through the grapevine that your father used to
pimp hoes.
I think It's funny.
That your prep school may have been paid for with some of that
wrong side of the tracks money.
My friends may come from the streets, been in jail and a lot even
killed,
But do you ever think that your friends hang with you just to keep
their quota filled?
You work for a Fortune 500 company,
Does that make you better than me?
You hang with your white preppy friends,
Does that make you better than me?
When I look in the mirror,
I know who I be.
When you look in the mirror,
I wonder who it is that you see?

TABOO

My father did get around,
He had seven children with six women around town.
Only two of us knew each other growing up,
That's what makes this situation so screwed up.
I saw her at the skating rink,
I was so enamored my eyes did not blink.
There was something so familiar about her,
Dag gone it.
I just couldn't put my finger on it.
Phone numbers were exchanged and now the relationship begins,
Three months later we were much more than friends.
This was the perfect collusion,
Until our father introduced us as brother and sister at the family
reunion.

BILLBOARDS

Driving down the streets I see billboards that read —
"Real men love babies."
"Don't leave kids in hot cars."
"Be fathers to your kids."
Do we need billboards to tell us this?
What the hell went wrong?

FUNNY BONE

Your husband bought you a new car, a new wardrobe and a new home,
Yet you say it's me that tickles your funny bone.
He is one hell of a provider,
But compared to him I look like a trash truck driver.
Even though you work at a cosmetic place,
You love the smile lines that I put across on your face.
You hate living in your 7-figure home,
Yet you love my place in the horrible zip code because I tickle your funny bone.
So now it's time to choose.
Will I lose?
Yep.
She chose to have her funny bone removed.
She didn't want the man that made her laugh,
Instead she chose the man that makes the cash.
Hmmmm.

WEDDING VOWS

It's the first day without my wedding ring and everything is calm.
But with it on, I had women shooting at me like it was Vietnam.
What is it about this gold circle that makes you want to shoot your shot?
If the tables were reversed, I'd risk getting shot.
Now, I'm not calling you a hoe,
But is your self-esteem really that low?
Are the pickings out there just that slim?
Take out your pent-up aggression at the gym.
Or a single guy named Jim.
Please do better and raise the bar,
Stop hollering at married men at the bar.

GLORIA

No matter how high the hill,
No matter how treacherous the terrain may be,
I must give a helping hand,
Because this child is a product of me.
You may wonder how it's possible for me to write so much,
Even though our personalities have only crossed just once.
By knowing your daughter,
I feel that I truly know you.
My intuition tells me,
That you did not raise a fool.
They say, "The apple doesn't fall far from its tree."
Your youngest child is so classy, elegant, and complete.
Someday I may be blessed to call her my wife.
I'm glad she was raised by a woman so strong, beautiful, and full of life.
Now I must focus all my attention on my unborn kid.
I'm willing to die for to give him the life I wish I'd lived.

ANESTHESIA

Ding Dong!
My doorbell rings.
It's the neighbor.
She has no clue that she's my flavor.
She's sweet and kind,
But I keep things above board.
I never want to be the creepy guy next door.
She said she just left the dentist and was feeling a bit loopy,
She said she wants to watch a porno movie.
She said she liked having sex from behind,
Now I know, she's not in her right mind.
She had on an extremely tight revealing t-shirt from the University
of Alabama.
She stepped into my kitchen and she did a trick with a banana.
Would I be taking advantage of this woman that's otherwise
classy?
Her speech is not slurred, and her eyes are not glassy.
Well shame on me,
But she did give me memories to savor.
At the next neighborhood block party,
I found out she used the same loopy dentist story on my neighbor.
So am I the creepy guy next door,
Or is she the next-door whore?

DON'T WANT ME

To all the men.
You don't want me in your life.
You don't want me in your wife.
I strongly suggest you treat that lady right.
Stop all your arguing and complaining night after night.
Pounding on your chest so hard,
Only leads to me pounding your wife so hard.
You don't want me in your life.
You don't want me in your wife.
You say it's only a little verbal abuse,
That's like telling a slave it's only a little noose.
You ask who in the hell do I think I am,
Well your wife is the biscuit and I'm the jam.
So, get your wedding vows right,
Because I might already be in your life.

FRIENEMIES

You were my only friend that was not a crook,
Now I'm writing my name in the guest book.
The guest book at your funeral,
At your childhood church.
In 43 minutes, we will lower you into the dirt.
You were in all the papers and on all the TV's.
Every picture they showed of you included me.
Side by side you didn't see one without the other.
Hand in hand I walk to the cemetery with your mother.
I have tears in my eyes,
So that people think this pain hurts.
But only God knows I killed you,
Putting you six feet under the dirt.

HURT PEOPLE, HURT PEOPLE

Follow a bully home and I bet you see him get bullied.
Hurt people, hurt people.
Police abuse and kill young Black men.
Hurt people, hurt people
Pedophiles molest and ravage innocent kids.
Hurt people, hurt people
Give your pain to God because we are all his people.

JOLLY RANCHER

I never thought that you and I would last past one week.
That's why I was in a hurry to get you between my sheets.
Boy was I wrong,
I had no clue my feelings would escalate this strong.
Now I'm having regrets about us committing that sin.
Now I'm wishing I could rewind time and simply start as friends.
That's the way the best relationships start off,
So hopefully our first sex date won't pre-destine this relationship
as a loss.

GROWN

I used to fight over street corners, neighborhoods, and blocks that
I didn't own,
Now I'm grown.
I used to argue with people because they were of a different race,
Now I'm grown.
Now I know it's your character,
Not the color of your face,
I used to run around with hoes,
Now I understand commitment and monogamy because I'm
grown.
My best friend goes every place I go.
We are joined at the hip because that's how we live.
Yet he still fights and cheats on his wife because he's still a kid.
So, to my childhood friends,
Don't think you have to leave me alone.
I'm just on another level,
Because I'm grown.

HOW?

How in the world did one hug reinvigorate my love?
Like you were the outlet and I'm the plug.
How in the world can you wish me well?
While hugging me from inside a jail cell.
How in the world are you able to forgive?
After what I did to you and your kids?
How in the world did you ask the judge to forgive my belligerence?
Also, my ignorance?
This was not a white-collar crime of internet hacking,
This was a ruthless carjacking.
"How in the world?"
God is not of this world.
That's how!

LOVE YOU, NOT

I want to learn how to use an Ouija board,
Or even learn how to tie a noose using an extension cord.
I want to purchase a shovel,
Then get up the nerve to ask for a favor from the devil.
I wish you would call me into the bathroom to give you a backrub,
And oops!
I trip and accidentally drop the blow dryer into the bathtub.
That hour I spent in between your legs was not worth all these
years of this BS.
I wish I had simply shot my load on your beautiful chest.

PONDER

Emotionally,
Oh god, I'm so attracted to you.
Spiritually,
Oh god, I'm so attracted to you.
Your heart and mind.
Hell, even the way you cook.
God, I'm so attracted to that.
You would make the perfect wife, but physically,
I'm so un-attracted to you.
Somebody help!
What do I do?

LOVE'S GONNA GET YOU

I typically don't like women with tattoos,
But, there's just something about you.
I love how you keep a pistol in your purse,
I love how you're real - like your words have not been rehearsed.
For some reason I love that your breath always smells like whiskey,
I guess you're my thug girl, Misty.
It turns me on to know that you once had a girlfriend,
When you spent those 8 months in the federal pen.
I love you and you love me,
But, I hate that you gave me HIV.

MIND

When she comes home 40 minutes late,
You're cussing her out.
(In your mind)
When she's leaving the house in yoga pants,
You're cussing her out.
(In your mind)
All her business trips from Houston to Indianapolis and in-
between,
You're cussing her out.
(In your mind)
Although she pays your alimony and child support,
Plus your lawyer and your charges from court.
As clueless as you are,
You're about to understand,
Because in two weeks she's leaving you for your cousin Pam.
(Not in her mind)
(In her reality)

MEN CHEAT?

Every man cheats.
Stop! Because that's weak.
A monogamous relationship I can undoubtedly cope,
So please don't paint all men with one broad stroke.
I'm sorry if you don't understand,
But I do believe in one woman one man walking hand in hand.
So, save your brush for your friends and many others.
I'm an individual,
Not paint by numbers.
A man will be a man,
That saying does not justify you having a concubine, harem, or a
clan.
I can do me and her, her and I without a doubt,
Keep my name out of your mouth.
Don't include me in the games you and your friends are playing,
If you know what I'm saying.

RECKLESS

She's so materialistic.
Reckless driving putting on her lipstick.
Putting on makeup on her way to work.
I don't see the need.
Now she's reckless driving on her way to the club, smoking weed.
Driving reckless with her boyfriend, Rob,
All while giving him a blow job.
She looked so good when she left the house,
Not wearing a seatbelt because she thought it would mess up her blouse.
Driving reckless, Rebecca is now dead
While texting and driving,
The steering wheel went through Rebecca's head.

CURSE

Did I Curse my sons with all the wrongs I've done?
I won't know until my demise.
If they will live their lives penalized.
Are they destined to fail,
Because I was destined for Hell?
Sometimes I think I see Evil behind their infant Eyes.
If they are cursed will their kids also inherit our wicked lives?
All in All the Question remains,
"How do I break the Chains?"

MY XXX

So, you think that everything is hunky dory,
But wait until they hear my side of the story.
How when we met you were sitting on top of a milk crate,
Because you just got evicted from Section 8.
That's where I made my mistake –
Taking you in.
I got your tattoos removed and introduced you to new friends.
No one had a clue that you were pathetic.
I took you out the strip club and cleaned up your credit.
You lived in gang infested neighborhoods,
Prostitutes and dogs constantly barking.
Now I have you going to steak houses and valet parking.
I tried to get you used to the opera,
But deep inside you were still addicted to the drama.
So, I'm going to let everyone know what this divorce is all about.
I'm letting them know,
I came home early and saw my sister's breast in your mouth.

MORE REGRETS

Hey wait!!!
I used to be a ghetto super star,
Now I'm duct taped in the trunk of this car.
I see the brake lights and I hear the music.
My life passes me by,
"Why did I abuse it?"
I used to go fishing, swim in the lake, and play little league sports.
God those summers were cut way too short.
I participated in Junior High School plays,
In all my advanced classes I made straight A's.
Then my parents stopped showing up to my baseball games.
That's when things started to change.
They stopped caring about my good grades.
That's when the drug dealers showed me how to make a little bit
of pocket change.
We stopped having family night, playing board games, and going
to Church.
Now I might trade in the trunk of this car for the back of a hearse.
They got divorced and forgot about me,
Now I'm trading in my love for them with my love for money.
It's not my fault that I was abandoned,
And used the streets as a stand in.
I start to cry and on myself I even start to pee,
I want a second chance to do right by that little boy that was me.
The car comes to a stop and the trunk opens.
I start wishing, praying, and hoping.
And next,
BANG!!!

SPRUNG

Me and the crew want to know when you will find your heart,
I know it must be like looking for a needle in the dark.
Do you have a cane with a red tip at the end,
Because you seem to be blind to all your friends.
You no longer accept our calls,
You seem to have lost your heart along with your balls.
How did a player like you get caught by a dictator?
If you want your balls back,
She keeps them in a drawer next to her vibrator.
You don't drink or watch sports.
Hell, you don't even curse.
The last time you were spotted,
You were at the mall holding her purse.
Man, she treats you like dirt.
We just want to know,
How you keep your penis from showing through your skirt.
I guess that's what love is all about.
Oh yea! Stop sipping your tea with your pinky finger stuck out.
Love ya man.

STALKER

I'm not sorry Black America.
I can't keep my silence,
About what's going on with this domestic violence.
Yes, I'm aware it goes on in the other community,
But right now, I'm talking to you and me.
He camped outside your house for days on end,
You don't know how it got here because you started off as friends.
He showed you so many red flags,
You didn't put them together,
Now it's July and you're wearing a turtleneck sweater.
Attempting to hide all the bruises and black marks,
You're nervous taking out the trash because it's dark.
Remembering when you two met?
You were so excited.
Now he shows up to family reunions, office parties and girl's night,
Uninvited.
He used to say, "he would die without you".
You thought it was funny.
Only now you know he was serious.
But his baby is in your tummy.
Guess who's showing up drunk at the baby shower?
Yep! Baby daddy/Stalker/Coward.
So, rock a bye baby on the treetop,
When the wind blows, baby mama just might get shot.
(Look for red flags ladies).

TAG

Make sure you know who you're dealing with,
Or else, TAG you're it!
Not hopscotch or double-dutch, she loves tag,
If you get caught, you might end up in a body bag.
She's a sexual freak.
Her game used to be hide & seek.
All it takes is her sensual kiss on your bottom lip,
And then tag you're it.
She knows how to twist and shake her butt, so it you must grab,
And then tag.
When she kisses you on the base of your neck,
Eventually it's something you may regret.
Once you're it,
This game you cannot quit.
This childhood game you do not want to play,
Because once you're tagged, she puts HIV in your DNA.
Beware because she's still on the loose,
So, you might just want to stick to duck-duck goose.

REFLECTIONS

Mirror, mirror on the wall,
Who's the fairest one of all?
"Not you."
I wish they made a mirror that told you the truth.
What looks great on her,
May not on you.
True.
Even though it may hurt,
Everyone was not meant to wear yoga pants or that mini skirt.
"Oh, yes I did."

NEAR DEATH

I thank you for being there for me,
Who else would, given our history?
With one call you were by my side,
When I didn't know whether I was dead or alive!
You've been the reason why I kept on believing.
After all the crazy situations and all the ridiculous things.
In troubled times you were the girl scout,
I was the bird with the broken wing.

GLORIFY

Why do we glorify the life of a thug?
The lifestyle of selling a drug.
A glorified grave digger.
Oh yea, like it's so hard to squeeze a trigger.
Why do we want to glorify a lifestyle that's nothing more than a
lie?
That lifestyle I too used to romanticize,
Until my best friend got murdered in front of my eyes.
When somebody gets shot,
We've made it into something sexy.
This is real life,
There are no credits rolling at the end of this movie.
What we need to glorify is a black man wearing a tie.
You bought into the lifestyle of being so hard,
Yet, you vomited uncontrollably when your sister got murdered at
the bar.
It's so easy to put on a hard face,
Until you're confronted with a murder case.
So, stay proud.
Stay strong and stand tall.
What you should glorify is putting a college diploma on your
mother's wall.

COWGIRL

We have had our ups and downs.
We have had our smiles and our frowns.
Through all the rain and all the pain.
Though I'm out of your life right now,
If you ever call - I'll be right back again.

Forever yours!

DARE

With a tear in my eye, I dared a dream to leave the hood.
Now I'm in Texas for thirteen plus years!
With a tear in my eye, I dared to dream to stop drinking.
Now I'm four plus years sober!
With a tear in my eye, I dared to dream to try to stop smoking.
Now I'm three plus years smoke free!
With a tear in my eye, I dared to get my G.E.D.
Now I have my GED, class A CDL, and class A barber license!
With a tear in my eye, I dared to dream to write a book.
Well now you're reading it!

I DARE YOU TO TRY!

I WILL BE

At my demise,
Sprinkle my ashes into the wind so that I am able to touch lives.
When you feel the wind blow it will be me.
When you extend your hand and touch a waterfall it will be me.
When you see a rainbow it will be me.
Because everything will be at my departure,
There will be no need to cry and wonder why.
I will be everything,
From the oak leaf that falls from the tree,
To the cumulus cloud in the sky.
I will be,
Because everything will be me.

Dedicated to Kristine

PAST LIFE

I love to clean, cook and take care of my son.
In my past life was I a housewife?
I love lifting weights in very close quarters, and movies about
prison.
In my past life was I in prison?
Maybe for a bad decision?
In the grocery store I love to see raw bloody meat,
In my past life was I a lion with the African soil under my feet?
How ironic that it's very simple to figure out my past,
Yet in this life I have no clue of what's the task.

BAD GUYS

So, you want to know about my life?
In the fifth grade, I was carrying a steak knife.
In Junior High, I was carrying a .22.
Then it was a sawed off shot gun by the time I went to High
School.
So, you want to know where it went from there?
Well I don't know how I avoided the electric chair.
Yet here you still sit,
Kissing my bottom lip.
I do not understand,
Why you're still here caressing my hand
I guess bad guys do finish first.
Sorry good fellas!

FRIENDS WITH BENEFITS

We are not kids,
Let's call it what it is.
You have your child, your career, and you're working on your
master's degree.
Out of seven days you can only fit half of a day in for me.
Between the homework for your child and yourself,
Our relationship has basically been put on the shelf.
You hate the saying "Friends with Benefits,"
Are you afraid of the stigma of being called a hoe or a bitch?
You are a career woman, single mom and so much more.
Never a hoe, basically a hero.
When the time is right everything will definitely come together.
The real definition of friends with benefits,
Is what I have with your mother "Heather."

YOU

I'm talking to a small percentage of you all.
The ones that boost clothes at the mall.
The ones that run credit card schemes.
The ones that hide their boyfriend's dope in the seams of their jeans.
The ones that get food stamps then they turn around and sell,
Then take that money and put it on your man's books in jail.
The ones that have your light bill in your child's name.
Basically, everybody that runs game.
I'm not saying it's wrong or right,
Just know that everything that's done in the dark will eventually come to light.

100%

Take my sight.
My hearing.
Even my physique.
And I will still be 100%,
Because you can never take my personality.

CALI GIRL

She's a white California girl,
That loves that down south black dick.
Her family members call her a bitch.
They call her a nigger lover.
She no longer talks to her father or mother.
I can only imagine how that makes her feel,
Especially when they cut her out of the family will.
Her parents are constantly playing the blame game.
They even asked her to disassociate herself from the family name.
All she wants is to be happy,
But that's unlikely as long as her man's hair is nappy.
She came over only to be told "never come back to their place."
Brittany went home and committed suicide,
All because of race.
Please stop the hate.

A LITTLE THANKS

Thanks whoever you are,
For praying for me,
For bringing me out of the darkness.
Now I am a Flame,
But you helped spark this!
Thanks for praying for me whoever you are.

TWO CRAZIES

I'm sitting in the bushes dressed up in camouflage,
In Aspen, Colorado outside the ski lodge.
It's January 10th, our anniversary.
Only problem is you're with him and not me.
I got tired of sitting in the basement listening to love songs,
Feeling as if you had done me wrong.
I hopped on an airplane,
I know it's insane.
Me and my bottle of Jim Beam,
Suddenly, I sensed somebody next to me.
I didn't know if it was a mirage,
It's a woman also in the bushes wearing camouflage.
She said that's her husband in the cabin with my wife,
I had a gun and she had a knife.
Both of our hearts were throbbing,
Then we found a mutual bonding.
That was one hell of a night.
Can you believe nine years later,
That lady ended up becoming my new wife?

VICE-VERSA

From devotion to deception.
From lust to lies.
How ironic you restored trust in me.
Consequently, you're the one that made it die.
There was a time when you were a cure,
For the pain that would not quit.
Funny how life plays its tricks,
Because now you're a part of it
Vice-Versa.

TIME TO TIME

I said, "I'm not looking for a commitment."
Just somebody to shoot the bull with.
(From time to time)
I can come by her house.
(From time to time)
I can put my hands down her blouse.
(From time to time)
From work we can play a little hooky.
(From time to time)
On our lunch break I can get a little nookie.
She said she wanted somebody to pay her mortgage,
Take her to the Bahamas so she can use her fancy luggage.
She wanted somebody to manicure her grass,
Yes, both meanings you dumb ass.
Life's a full circle because again I couldn't commit,
So, from time to time I guess two people can have an amicable
split.

LIFE'S TRICKS

1st period, I'm in high school under the bleachers with the prom
queen.
Who knew in a few years she would be a dope fiend?
2nd period, I'm out back sneaking cigarettes with the class clown,
Who knew in a few years he would be the mayor of our
hometown?
3rd period, I'm in study hall getting tutored by the school geek,
Who knew she'd turn out to be a porn star, an undercover freak?
4th period, I'm cutting class with the high school whore,
Whoever knew she'd end up as a nun looking like the girl next
door?
You want to know whatever happened to the high school thug,
gangster, crook?
Here's a hint –
You're reading my book
You never know who is going to turn out to be who in high school
life,
The person you're sitting next to m.ay turn out to be your wife.
Or the person that takes your life,
You see, that's the high school life.

PIECES

I write this poem in the blood from my heart that you once broke,
The Pain and Sorrow is in every turn of this pen and every stroke.
All the questions of why and all the love that was lost,
is in every 'I' that I dot and every 'T' that is crossed.
All the screaming nights and all the drama,
Is represented in every Exclamation Mark and every Comma.
When I erase my mistakes and brush the small rubber fragments
off the paper,
The Fragments represent the pieces of my shattered heart I hope
to put back together.
Sooner rather than Later!

GULLIBLE

He used to have a soft spot in his heart for prostitutes, strippers,
even the occasional whore,
He always tried to turn them into the girl next door.
He often bought every sad story that they would tell,
He drained his bank account paying their rent, car payments, and
even their bail.
He's been burnt so often,
That now he has a soft spot for putting them in a coffin.

TRACI

Since my birth in 1970,
There are so many buildings claiming to be heavenly.
There are so many churches in this neighborhood,
Claiming things will eventually be good.
It's been 49 years,
However, my hood has become overrun with tears.
Do I abort ship?
Do I simply quit?
My hood has slowly declined,
Simultaneously these churches have inclined.
I wonder,
"Is this God or the devil putting these thoughts in my mind?"
Pretend this poem is a tape cassette.
Hit rewind three times.
Think?

BLACK MAN

You say a percentage of us are incarcerated.
You say a percentage of us are Gay.
I am neither, yet you won't give *me* the time of Day!
Hmmm.

DEPENDENT

Where's the woman to take the place of sips?
Where's the woman to take the place of the puffs?
When I find her will I come to depend on her too much?
Will I use her like a crutch?

THE MAN

Are you the man that tells your wife on Mother's Day,
"You're not my mother?"
Are you the man that tells your wife that you never had a father,
Because of that, you don't know how to be a father.
Are you the man that buys your wife discount flowers and candy,
The day after Valentine's Day?
Are you the man that took an extra shift at work,
To work on your wife's birthday?
Are you the man that wonders why I'm sleeping with your wife?

SOMETHING ABOUT MARY

On the first day of his son's school registration,
He picked up on a vibe from a heavenly creation,
But it would be perpetration.
He gets a call that night thinking it's to go over his son's
curriculum,
Only what he heard on the phone almost made him cum.
It was the lady from today's school registration.
So his vibe wasn't perpetration,
She was flirting with no hesitation.
She said that she felt she got her calling at the age of eight,
Now she's 2nd, 3rd and 4th guessing her faith.
She said for the three hours we met,
There was a connection that she would do something she might
regret.
He said he will be at her job at noon,
He paid the janitor to lend him the key to the utility room.
In case it's not obvious, yes this will be a nooner.
Some people think it's immoral that he's screwing her.
She herself said she can't resist him and whispers in his ear,
"You're a fool."
Because she's the head nun at his son's catholic school.
After he nailed Mary,
He said three Hail Mary's.

YOU ARE WHAT YOU ARE

You are what you are,
And that's due to no fault of your own.
They say God don't make junk,
So I left it alone.
As time went on,
So many things I could not deny.
I stopped.
Added it up and realized,
(That saying is just another lie)
You are what you are!!
God does make junk.

MESSAGE IN A BOTTLE

God tell me where's my wife?

A.K.A my angel.

Please send her to me.

Someone who doesn't have the capability to lie,

Someone that I don't have the capability to make cry.

Someone that makes me count the minutes until she calls,

Even if all we have to say is nothing at all.

Lord can you intertwine our hearts – such as someone with a needle and thread knits,

So when I meet my angel it's guaranteed our souls will be a perfect fit.

A woman that makes me want to bow down and ask for her hand from her father.

I close my eyes as I throw it into the water.

My message in a bottle.

666

I was in the fight of my life,
Only God brought me through those crazy nights.
Going through so many things that were intolerable,
I came across the bible.
Then, I became unstoppable.
Then she came across my path,
So, I did the math.
Her plus me equals greatness,
So, I approached her with wariness and shakiness.
It was instant fireworks like puppy love from Junior High School.
The day went so well,
I'm surprised we didn't end the night with matching tattoos.
All of a sudden things took a dive into the dirt,
When I asked her to accompany me the next day to church.
She told me that she practices Wiccan,
If you don't know what that is,
Look up the definition.

BRIGETTE

Hey! Hey! Hey!
Do you remember me?
Hell yeah, you were the prom queen.
My teenage dream.
I was just the high school thug.
I never would have imagined that you and I would be embraced in
a hug.
People gave us awkward glances,
While we reminisced about her red BMW and me fighting at the
school dances.
The car behind me honked the horn,
I gave her my spare change and hit the gas because I had to move
on.

IT'S NOT ME, IT'S YOU

I made a list and I'm checking it twice.
Looking at all the women that's come into my life that could have
been my wife.
They all were God-fearing, loyal, stylish, plus a college degree.
I need to look in the mirror because the problem is obviously me.
When I glanced in the mirror and seen what was looking back,
They were the problem because I am all that.
My looks and success will never go to my head.
"Well, that's all the time we have for today,"
Is what my therapist said.

CYCLE

I'm a circle peg and you're a square block,
Why do you keep trying to make it fit when it's obviously not!
How long apart this time?
2 Months?
6 Months?
A Year?
Why do we keep torturing ourselves, I think it's out of fear.
Why can't we leave each other alone?
Is it because nobody wants to be alone?
Will we keep this up until there's nothing left?
Or will we finally kill each other and together we will be side by
side each other in Death?

2009

Today I saw a homeless man die from dehydration,
Yet they found water on the moon yesterday.
Now that's perpetration.

PTS

I'm one of the few that made it out of my neighborhood,
Why do I feel guilty about living good?
It feels wrong – buying nice things for my home.
Sometimes I wonder, "Do I have Post Treatment Syndrome?"
It feels great when I purchase something nice, I can't lie,
I know it can be taken away in the blink of an eye.
Maybe I'm simply out of my league.
Maybe I should just move back to those eastside streets where
most of my partners are buried;
I guess the change is scary.
I might have to watch my back and behind,
Ironically enough, I might have a piece of mind.

FUN

She's fun,
But she's not the one.
When the sun's up, she's so uptight,
When the moon's out, she does the things most women think
aren't right.
She does magic tricks with her mouth,
She's also a magician with my bank account.
She makes money appear where before there was none,
If I'm in need, she never treats me like a vampire treats the sun.
She's fun, but she's not the one.
Financially – Yes.
Sexually – Yes.
But there's just too much damage on the inside of her chest.

CAJUN LOVIN'

I'm still in the hospital because two days ago,
My ex-girl left this note on my car window.
"Hey, Man-hoe! I put pubic hairs in your Gumbo!"

VOYEURISM

You didn't think I'd notice the spy cameras that you put in my home?
Is it strange that it turned me on?
I knew you were watching me from the other side,
On your laptop, your home theatre, or even in your ride.
Yes, that was a red flag that you're crazy;
Although I imagined you masturbating to me in your Mercedes.
To my surprise the police knocked at my door.
Come to find out, it was your husband that installed cameras behind my doors.

BROTHERLY LOVE

Stranded for two days in Alabama,
All because of a blizzard back home in Indiana.
I couldn't wait to see my wife on that frigid Friday,
Strangely, I noticed the most exotic tire marks in my driveway.
I shrugged it off.
Just trying to get to my lady with this wine and put these logs on
the fire in the loft.
Obviously, I was yet to understand,
That Spring I seen the same exotic tire prints at a family funeral in
the sand.
Later that Summer I saw the same exotic tire marks on my
brothers' hummer.
Why was Matt at my house with my wife during a snowstorm?
I found out months later when my son was born.

GOOD OLE DAYS OR NOT

I've had police chases.
I've been through hard knock towns.
I've had my ups and my downs.
At age thirteen I mastered breaking a car window without making
any noise.
Much more ruthless than just your neighborhood boys!
Saturday afternoon at the mall while you would shop,
I was out raiding your car in the parking lot!
Sunday mornings while you were in church praising God,
Once again I'm trying to steal the hub caps off the Cadillac,
minivans, or hot rods!
I've came a long way from those days of insanity.
But I still ask the Lord to forgive me.
But those were the times.
The times that replay in my mind!

GREY SKIES

Rain drops drip from the gutter,
Rain beats hard against my shutter.
Rain, rain don't go away,
Why won't you stay every day?
Why is it the sun I hate so much?
I can't wait for the moon rays to descend onto my skin and touch.
Moon up to moon down and night in to night out,
A picnic in the park after dark is what I'm talking about!
Overcast, cloudy skies,
Oh what a beautiful day in my eyes!
A mist of water sprays off tires as cars roll through the streets,
A perfect day for only me and maybe a leech.
Rain, rain don't go away!
Stay another day so I can play!

BROKE

Born broke with no hope.
Living in the Section 8 side of my city.
Not even milk came out of my mother's titty.
Being laughed at was almost too much,
Because in Elementary I received free lunch.
But wait!
These are just the rules of society.
I'm not broke even though I have no money.
I have parents, grandparents, and even a great-grandmother.
All the money in the world couldn't buy how much I love her.
So being broke is just a state of mind,
All I have to do is simply look behind.
The people that have my back are my uncles and cousins,
No amount of money can pay that tuition of lovin'.
So, if you think that you're broke,
Check your support system.
If you believe nothing else,
Please believe my wisdom.

HOPE

Who laughs at my jokes?
You do.
Who smiles when I call?
You do.
Who listens when I tell long stories?
You do.
Who puts a different perspective on life?
You do.
Who gives me something to look forward to?
You do.
Maybe one day I can have the honor of hearing her say, "I do."

THOUGHTS

I used to write misspelled graffiti on the walls,
I used to have one hand on my bottle and the other on my balls.
I used to ride from hood to hood looking for the best marijuana,
Just me and my homegirl Tawana.
I used to steal money from my mother's purse,
I used to smoke weed before church.
I used to have sex with whores without a condom,
I used to see people with nice things then I would rob them.
I used to be proud of the stories I'd tell,
My friends hung on to every word about my time in jail.
Anyone can change.
Trust me this is so true,
My life changed when I fell in love with you,
Over the summer of 1992.
This is personal,
I know it makes no sense to you.

UNSEEN

Take the blindfold from my eyes,
Now I can see.
(Wow)
The world is an ugly place,
Put the blindfold back on me.

DOUBTS

Are you the one that cheats on your wife?
The one that sneaks out to sleep with other men at night?
Are you the grown man that touches little kids,
Yet, you're in church every Sunday rebuking others' sins?
Are you the one with prostitutes in your sheets?
Are you the one selling dope to the youth on the streets?
Are you the one lying next to the one I'm talking about?
Don't be sure, if you have any doubts.
Any doubts...
Any doubts...
Any doubts...

QUIET AS KEPT

This is the last time I'm going to allow you to cuss me out.
This is the last time I'm going to stand here and listen to those
words come out of your mouth.
I'm about to do what I said I never would do,
But, finally telling you this is the only way to shut you up for good.
Every time you told me I wasn't worth a damn,
I had someone telling me that I'm the man.
Every time you told me you would be there to spit on my grave
the day I get buried,
I had someone telling me she wishes I was the one that she
married.
Every time you were screaming that I can't never do a damn thing
right,
I had someone saying that I'm the love of her life.
For so long on my heart I thought you put a permanent blister,
But funny how it healed when I fell in love.
Yes, me and your sister.

FORTUNE

Today I saw a man robbing a store across the street.
So, I waited.
Then I robbed him.
Old habits die hard.

FORGOTTEN

She's been waiting her whole life for her calling,
But that call never came.
I guess her phone was OFF the hook,
Because her phone never rang
She thought she was doing good for so many years on end,
But it was a false sense of security because she was only doing
better than her loser friends.
Now out in the real world she feels like she has no help,
Maybe GOD took her dreams and put them on a shelf.
Tucked far, far away covered in dust,
Maybe that's why her life is filled with bad luck.
Forgotten like an old child's toy.
Man-o-man, Boy-o-boy.

LITERALLY

I do mean this literally.
Please expand your vocabulary.
Mix in a noun or a verb.
Everything out of your mouth does not need to be the "N" word.
So again, please expand your vocabulary.
Again, I do mean that literally!

MEDIOCRE

I'm not here to be mediocre,
I'm striving to be a killer whale – not your run of the mill fish like a
croaker.
It will take me some time because I move in slow motion,
Patience is a virtue – soon I will be the king of this ocean.
God personally molded me like an artist sculpts a lump of clay,
So I strive to avoid mediocracy when my alarm clock awakens me
every day.

MISS AMERICA

Miss America pageant is based off your looks.
You need to quit.
I would love to see a Miss America pageant based off intelligence
and wit.

KIM

Kim heard the neighbor say,
"Hey, I didn't see you in church yesterday."
Kim thought that her answers would come quicker from a bottle
of liquor.
The neighbor said,
"Hey, I'll see you in the prayer meeting tomorrow I hope."
Once again Kim thought she will get the answers quicker from
smoking dope
Well on the upside, Kim finally made it to church.
On the downside, it was in a hearse.
The bible says come as you are,
But, you don't want to come in that long black car.

FUTURE WIFE

My House is immaculate, my car is astounding
I have nothing but fine women around me.
My son is a God sent and my baby mama is cool,
But the only thing missing in my life is you!
I've held auditions state to state, like American Idol,
And still I can't find a woman to give the title.
I've spent nine months' worth of money to rent a search light.
It shines night after night
And still no wife!

HALF CRAZY

I talk to myself because I'm the only one that can truly
understand,
I don't fit the stereotype of a man.
Hard yes, strong yes, and I love a woman's head laying on my
chest.
Yet, sometimes I still cry late at night,
As I talk to myself and wonder why.
So much potential,
Yet so much wasted.
As I talk to myself all I can hear is hatred.
"Will I end up on the streets?"
Thinking to myself out loud,
As strangers give sympathy looks,
While I pass by a crowd.
This is how I speak from my heart,
I wonder,
"Is this how it starts?"

NEVER QUIT

To their surprise I rise and stand up from the grave,
Such as Jesus did on the 7th day.
Men thought I was buried, gone, and my soul had diminished,
At the same time women left me because they thought I was
finished.
I heard a thousand questions curious and asking "Why?"
It's simple, a man like me will never die.
I'm back, bigger, badder, and stronger.
Now on my second time around,
The lord has promised me that my reign will surely be longer.
I never give up - like the sun forcing its rays through the clouds.
I will be heard - like a baby bird's voice chirping out loud.

BRUISES

I wanted to make love,
She secretly wanted to be screwed.
I wanted to love her,
She secretly wanted to be misused.
I wanted to take her out on the town,
She secretly wanted to be smacked around.
Being treated like a rag doll was so common placed,
It was normal to look in the mirror, only to see a bruise on her face
Well a lesson learned –
Never get with a woman that thinks being treated bad is what she
deserves.

MR. ANONYMOUS

Mr. Anonymous,
It was me hiding on the side of the liquor store,
Waiting for you to exit your car door.
Only it was me that had no clue of what you had in store.
At 15 years old I asked you to buy me a drink,
Mr. Anonymous, you didn't hesitate, nor did you blink.
You pulled me aside and explained the path my life was heading down,
I couldn't give a damn - I thought about putting you 6-feet underground.
You see that was my mentality,
But years later looking back at my life,
I realized that Mr. Anonymous was right.
So, thanks for giving a spiritual hug to a thug.
Whoever you are.

DEAD END

I'm the son of a son of a son of a slave,
And now on my back are all their graves.
I was never taught that you can grow up to be anything you want
to be,
So, I grew up trying to be the things I would see.
I saw the drunk, the dope head, the hoe, and the gangster,
At the time I wasn't anything but a pre-teen prankster.
Once again that was all that my young eyes have seen,
I never even heard of an all-black college until the age of 19.
I was going a hundred and fifty miles per hour on a dead-end
street.
Nobody tried to stop me –
The teachers, the neighbors, not even the police
Not even my family did much to stop me from becoming this mad
man
Or try to put a stop to the devil's plan.
They could have done more,
They didn't do all that they can.
Street hustlers as role models,
My trophies are beer bottles.
Going a hundred and fifty miles an hour on a dead-end street,
And I just hit the gas throttle.

REMINISCING

There are no more romantic movies.
There are no more love songs.
You can call me old,
Maybe that's where things started to go wrong?

S.L.D.

I kept her a secret, undercover and under wraps,
Because I didn't know how all the others would react.
It took a virtual stranger to let me know that my heart needed
help,
Then came the stranger's words,
"That I was only hurting myself."
Just a few observant words let me know it wasn't wrong,
My heart screamed so loud because I knew it was true.
Yet my mind chose to ignore it,
So, my mind made me a fool.
For so long this angel stood by,
But, my mind won the battle over my heart and made me blind.
A short time later I no longer had the privilege of calling her mine.
I often rewind our relationship in my head as if it were a tape,
Who says that a mind is a terrible thing to waste?

THUG RAP

I Live with my Mama.
I don't have a Car.
I have two kids by two different women.
I'm short and my Belly Protrudes.
But damn you're Fine,
So I'm going for Broke because I don't have a thing to lose.
I only can stand to Gain.
You look so good in that dress,
If I'm Lucky Tonight you can be my Monica Lewinski and on that
dress I can leave a Stain.
Did that make you laugh?
Did that make you giggle?
At least for a minute I cracked that stuck up exterior,
Bringing you back down to Earth just a little.
Would you buy the line,
"I have a see-through waterbed at home with fish in it?"
Oh, I see I made you Smile again.
But no, I'm just bull-shittin'!
Well you gave me your number,
Girl that's a Surprise!
Even after all those BS lines.
Let's see 876-Go-2-Hell-Fool.
HA-HA I see you got Jokes too!

I'M BACK

I'm back.
To my sisters whose skin tone is black,
Answer me this...
Will you welcome me back even though I crossed the fence?
Blonde hair, red hair, and brunettes.
Yes, I've endured much fun, yet many regrets.
Eyes of blue, eyes of green,
Maybe it was the opposites attract thing that may have tempted
me.
They say that grass is greener but it wasn't all grass,
It was also the green of the money.
Subconsciously, that may have played a part in them looking so
lovely.
We could talk about this fetish all day turning it into a debate.
To put it simply, on so many levels,
Her and I just couldn't relate.
Now don't get me wrong snowflake,
For you in my heart there will always be a place,
I just don't think that anymore it's my acquired taste.
My sisters, my sisters, you wanted me to explain,
All I can say is it was just one of those thangs.
Just Joking!
Or am I?
Hmmm.

WORDS HURT

So, you're the woman that's trying to put me in my place,
But you're the one caught in-between a rock and a hard place.
Listen you ghetto chick,
Using Vaseline on your chapped lips for lipstick.
Let's get something straight,
Before I talk about you paying $87.00 for rent because you're on Section 8,
It seems you have enough on your plate.
You claim that you know me,
You put so much energy into telling people I'm a phony.
Why not put that energy into finding your baby daddies –
Paul, Corey, Stacy, Lamont and Tony?
Didn't your momma have sex with your 3rd baby daddy at vacation bible study?
Then with your bi-sexual buddy?
Oh, I remember you now,
You're the one at tax time,
That asked me to claim your child.
WOW!
That's fire I just extinguished.
You see, it's possible to curse someone out without using curse language.
YOU MOTHA FUCKING HOE ASS BITCH!!

BOOGIE MAN

I can tell you where the boogie man hangs out,
Just find a place where somebody has a joint or a crack pipe up to
their mouth.
Oh yes I can show you where to find the boogie man,
Just find a place where a man is about to cheat on his woman –
Or a woman is about to cheat on her man.
Do you ever wonder,
Why some women wake up with make up?
Why some women wear cosmetics 24/7 every day?
Because you might find the boogie man under her Mary Kay.
He's in a place where death goes to die,
A place tears go to cry.
I know it's incomparable.
How do I know where to find the boogie man?
Let's just say,
Birds of a feather flock together.

RUDE AWAKENING

Realizing I choose women that are broken,
Is it because I'm broken?

BLACK MAN SHORTAGE

You know about the pain I've inflicted.
You know that my heart is truly wicked.
Yet, you still want to kick it.
(Black man shortage)
You know I detest wearing condoms.
You heard about my HIV scare,
Yet, you don't seem to care.
(Black man shortage)
You know about my eight kids with eight different ladies,
You know I'm a drug dealer and that's how I got my Mercedes.
You know I'm crazy or bi-polar some may call it.
You know that I'm an alcoholic.
You see all the pain I will put you through,
And yet last night you still asked me to marry you.
(Black man shortage)
I drop you off at your job in your car,
Then parade around the streets like a ghetto superstar.
Now it's after five o'clock and in front of your job you sit and wait.
Because even though it's your car, I still have the audacity to be
late.
(Black man shortage)

GOING DOWN

I bob up, I sink under!
I bob up, I sink under!
I know they see me, why won't they help, I wonder?
Almost disconnecting my shoulder
Trying to extend my hand
No one wants to take hold
I don't understand.
I go down, I come up, I see friends
I go down, I come up, I see family
Are they willing to stand by and watch this travesty?
Is this the thanks I get from all of y'all?
To stand by and watch me drown
In this sea of alcohol?
Each time I resurface for air
I get a glimpse of people that don't seem to care
Once again, I see family and friends
The current is sweeping me under
This is the end!
Seconds before I black out
I swear on some of their faces
I see a grin!

CPS

I walk with a limp because my mothers' boyfriend tried to shoot her,
But the bullet went into my hip.
I stutter because her next boyfriend pushed me down the ladder,
While cleaning out the gutters.
I lost partial vision in my left eye when her last boyfriend hit me in it,
All because I started to cry.
But I really, really, really like her new love.
Her name is Candice.
She's definitely the bestest.

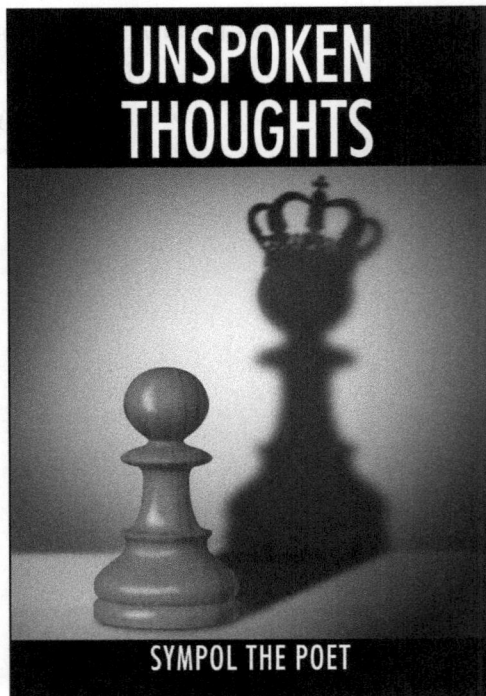

www.ingramcontent.com/pod-product-compliance
Lightning Source LLC
Chambersburg PA
CBHW060548100426
42742CB00013B/2493